BECOME AN
ELECTRICIAN

by Kate Conley

BrightPoint Press

San Diego, CA

BrightP◇int Press

© 2021 BrightPoint Press
an imprint of ReferencePoint Press, Inc.
Printed in the United States

For more information, contact:
BrightPoint Press
PO Box 27779
San Diego, CA 92198
www.BrightPointPress.com

LIBRARY OF CONGRESS CATALOGING-IN-PUBLICATION DATA

Names: Conley, Kate A., 1977- author.
Title: Become an electrician / Kate Conley.
Description: San Diego, CA : ReferencePoint Press, 2021. | Series: Skilled and vocational trades | Includes bibliographical references and index. | Audience: Grades 10-12
Identifiers: LCCN 2020003754 (print) | LCCN 2020003755 (eBook) | ISBN 9781678200121 (hardcover) | ISBN 9781678200138 (eBook)
Subjects: LCSH: Electrical engineering--Vocational guidance--Juvenile literature. | Electricians--Juvenile literature.
Classification: LCC TK159 .C66 2021 (print) | LCC TK159 (eBook) | DDC 621.319/24023--dc23
LC record available at https://lccn.loc.gov/2020003754
LC eBook record available at https://lccn.loc.gov/2020003755

CONTENTS

AT A GLANCE

- Electricians install electrical systems. They also maintain these systems. They work in a variety of settings.

- People who train to be electricians are called apprentices. Apprentices need on-the-job training. Sometimes they also take classes.

- Apprentices earn money while they learn their trade.

- Apprentices take an exam to earn a license. This license lets them work as electricians. Licensed electricians are called journey workers. With more training, they can become master electricians.

- Working with electricity can be risky. Electricians must pay attention to safety measures.

- Most electricians are good at working with their hands. Most are also physically fit and have good people skills.

- Electrician jobs are expected to increase by 10 percent between 2018 and 2028.

- People are using more renewable energy. This creates new jobs for electricians.

WHY BECOME AN ELECTRICIAN?

" I was good at math and science and was interested in electricity," recalls Gina Addeo.[1] Addeo is a master electrician. She grew up around electricians. Her father, Richard Addeo, was an electrician. He owned a small business that did electrical work.

Electricians may work together as part of a business.

As a teen, Addeo spent lots of time at her dad's business. Addeo soon realized she wanted to learn the trade too. "I knew I wanted to do something in the electrical industry, and I found it interesting. I admired

Electricians make sure equipment is installed properly and is safe to use.

my dad, and I wanted to help him,"

she says.[2]

Addeo earned her **license** as an

electrician. She became the first female

master electrician in New York City.

During her career, she has done many jobs. Some were small, such as installing wire. Others were large, such as planning a security system in a large airport. Today, she is a leader in the industry.

Addeo is one of more than 715,000 electricians in the United States. Electricians perform an important job for their communities. They install and maintain electrical systems. They make sure homes, schools, and businesses have power. They also make sure these systems are safe.

Working as an electrician is a trade. It is a type of work that requires special training.

Students must study hard to become successful electricians.

Electricians must take classes. They must

also learn from experienced electricians

while on the job. It takes several years to

complete the training. Students can then earn a license to work on their own. After gaining experience, some electricians start their own small businesses.

The job outlook for electricians is positive. Demand for qualified electricians is strong. Many parts of the country have a shortage of electricians. As a result, electricians are often well paid and in high demand. This is attracting many new students to the trade. It is a growing industry with many opportunities.

CHAPTER ONE

WHAT DOES AN ELECTRICIAN DO?

E lectricians work with electricity. Electricity is a type of energy. It can be collected and sent through wires. When a device is plugged into the wires, it receives power.

People first began to collect electrical power successfully in the 1880s.

Thomas Edison showed the benefits of electricity. Now electricity is widely used.

One of the leaders in the field was

Thomas Edison. He experimented with

electric light bulbs. Edison's experiments

led to other improvements. By 1925, half

of American homes had electricity. This increase created a demand for electricity experts. The result was a new job: the electrician.

Today, electricians work in many settings. Some work in new buildings. They install electrical systems using plans. Others repair existing systems. They figure out what is causing a problem in the system and fix it. No matter where they work, electricians make sure people have power.

INSTALLING ELECTRICAL SYSTEMS

New buildings all have electrical systems. These systems power lights and machines.

People rely on them every day. Electricians install these systems during construction. First, they connect the new building to the area's power supply. This supply is often called a power grid. It sends electricity through overhead or buried wires.

POWER GRIDS

The power grid begins at a power plant. A power plant is where electricity is made. Power plants create electricity in generators. The electricity made by generators is **high voltage**. It flows through heavy-duty cables, called power lines. These cables deliver electrical power to **transformers**. Transformers convert the electricity to a lower voltage. This lets customers use it safely. Homes, schools, and businesses connect to local transformers. This is how they receive electricity.

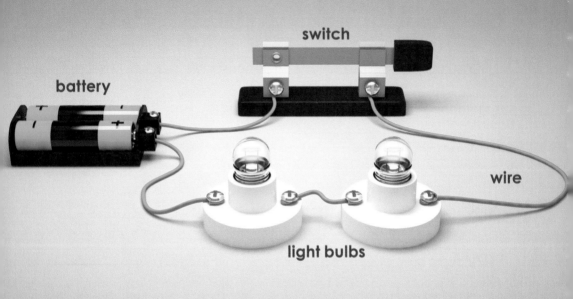

battery

switch

wire

light bulbs

Switches can interrupt the flow of electricity.

Electricians connect a new building to the power grid during construction. To do this, they install a meter. The meter shows how much electricity a building uses. They also install a main power switch. The main power switch has two jobs. It protects the building from **power surges**. It also separates the building's electrical system into **circuits**.

Electricians work with circuits every day. A circuit is a path that carries electricity. A simple circuit has three main parts. The first is a power source, such as a battery. The second is the device that uses the electricity, such as a radio. The third part is wires. These connect the battery to the radio. Most circuits also have switches. These turn the power on and off. Circuits send electricity to different parts of the building.

Electricians must run wires throughout the house before the walls go up.

With the circuits in place, electricians can move on to the next step. They install wires, outlets, and switches in the building. This step is part of construction's rough-in phase. The rough-in happens after a building's frame goes up. But it happens before the walls and ceilings are closed. This lets electricians and other workers easily access all parts of the building. Jeffrey Tyson is an electrician. He says that after the frame goes up, "we follow through with all of our wiring and conduits."[3]

When the rough-in is complete, workers put up the walls. At that point, "all of our

hard work gets hidden behind the walls,"
says Tyson. "But without all that important
rough-in work, nothing else can happen."[4]

READING BLUEPRINTS

During the rough-in, electricians refer to
blueprints. Blueprints are technical drawings
of a building. Architects and engineers
create blueprints. All of the people who
work on a building use its blueprints.
The blueprints are their guide for how to
build the building.

Blueprints and other technical drawings
give construction workers details about
the building. They tell electricians

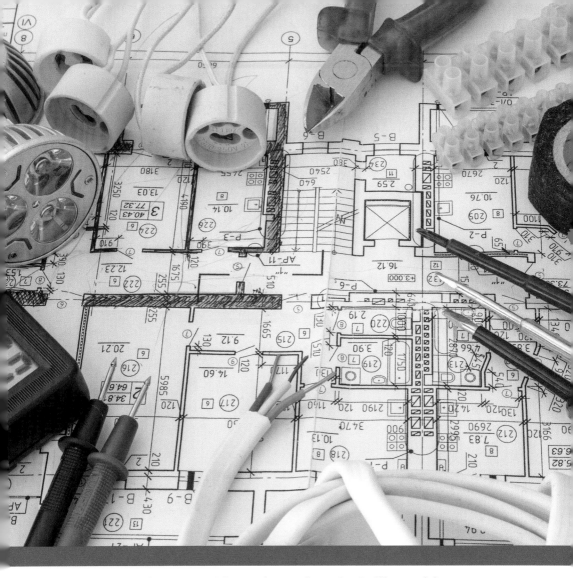

Electricians use blueprints when installing wiring and connecting electrical components.

where to place lights, switches, and

outlets. Blueprints also show how the

parts of the electrical system connect

Inspectors take a careful look at electrical work to make sure it can be safely used.

to each other. These parts are called

electrical components.

Electricians must know how to read

blueprints. The electrical components on a

blueprint are often written as symbols. Each element has its own symbol. One example is a push button, such as a doorbell. It is drawn as a square. The square has a black circle inside it. When electricians see that symbol on the blueprint, they know where to place the push button.

Electricians use blueprints mostly during the rough-in. Once the rough-in is complete, inspectors arrive. They check the electrical work. Inspectors make sure the electricians followed the blueprints properly. They also make sure the electrical work follows local and national laws. These laws are called electrical codes. The codes protect buildings. For example, poor wiring can cause fires.

After the inspector approves the work, the walls go up in the building. Electricians then return. They do the finishing work. It is the last stage of the construction process. It usually involves installing light fixtures, ceiling fans, and light switches. When this is complete, the electrical system is ready to use.

MAINTAINING ELECTRICAL SYSTEMS

Not all electricians work on new buildings. Many maintain buildings that already exist.

Electricians have to identify which part of an electrical system is broken. Then they can make repairs.

Sometimes a lot of work needs to be done.

An entire building may need to be rewired.

Old wiring may create a fire hazard. New

electrical systems make a home safer.

Old electrical systems may not work as

well as new ones. They were not created to

LINE INSTALLERS AND REPAIRERS

Not all electricians work in buildings. Some work with the power grid. They handle power coming from power plants. These electricians are called line installers and repairers. Line installers string overhead power lines. They also dig trenches to bury power cables. Line repairers help when the system has problems. For example, an overhead line might fall during a storm. This can cause power outages. Line repairers fix the problem and restore power.

support new technology. Today, people use more electricity than in the past. Laptops, cell phones, and televisions all require power. Old electrical systems may not be able to handle these heavy demands. Electricians can rewire a home. Then the home can easily handle the increased power demands.

In some cases, a home may have a light switch or outlet that stops working. Owners call electricians to fix the problem. This can be a difficult job. It is difficult because most wiring is hidden behind walls. It is not easy to see what is causing the problem. Many electricians enjoy this challenge of the job.

"Solving electrical problems can be like playing detective," says electrician Michael Lucas. Sometimes a house can have electrical problems from a single loose wire. To fix the problem, electricians must locate it. "These [loose wires] aren't easy to find, as they can be located in the switchbox, an outlet, a light fixture, in the attic, in the panel, at the meter, or even out by the city," says Lucas. "As an electrician you really have to think logically in order to figure it out."[5] Problem-solving is a key part of an

Some electricians enjoy figuring out where a problem is coming from.

electrician's job. Electricians use this skill

to keep homes, schools, and businesses

working properly.

CHAPTER TWO

WHAT TRAINING DO ELECTRICIANS NEED?

There are several steps to becoming an electrician. Electrician students must be at least eighteen years old. They must also have a high school diploma. Or they must pass the General Educational Development (GED) test. The GED tests whether a

Becoming an electrician requires thousands of hours of training.

person has a high-school-level education.

Then students begin an apprenticeship.

An apprenticeship is on-the-job training.

Many apprenticeships also include classes at a trade school. Trade schools prepare students for a specific job. The apprenticeship period for an electrician lasts between four and five years. The total length depends on the specific program.

APPRENTICE ELECTRICIANS

Unions and businesses provide apprenticeship programs. As apprentices, students work alongside licensed electricians. Students usually work as apprentices for forty hours a week. As part of their training, many apprentices attend evening classes. These classes may take

Apprenticeships allow new electricians to develop their skills and learn from more experienced electricians.

place two or three times a week. Class

requirements vary by program.

Apprentices learn many skills. In their first year, they study how electricity works. They learn how to read blueprints. Students become familiar with tools. They also learn safety measures. Later, they learn more difficult tasks. They learn how to build circuits and install fuses. Fuses are devices in an electrical circuit that cut off power if something goes wrong. By the

ELECTRICAL THEORY

Electrical theory is the study of how electricity works. Students learn the properties of electricity. They also learn electrical calculations and safety practices. Mastering this can take many years.

end of the apprenticeship, students are working on complex systems. They know how to calculate a load. A load is the amount of electricity a circuit can handle safely. Students also learn how to install transformers. During this time, apprentices learn from experienced electricians. Many of an electrician's skills are best taught on the job.

Being an apprentice has many benefits. Apprenticeships allow students to discover quickly whether they like the work. They can know before they graduate. Additionally, apprentices get paid as they learn. Their pay is typically 60 percent of what a licensed electrician earns. An apprenticeship is different from a four-year-college experience. Those students must pay to go to school. Many are in debt after they graduate. However, many apprentices finish their training without debt.

JOURNEY WORKER ELECTRICIANS

An apprenticeship generally requires 8,000 hours of training. These hours happen on the job. Training takes around four years. Apprentices may also spend about 300 hours in the classroom. After completing the hours, they take an exam. They earn

Journey worker electricians can perform certain repairs on their own.

Average Annual Wage of Electricians

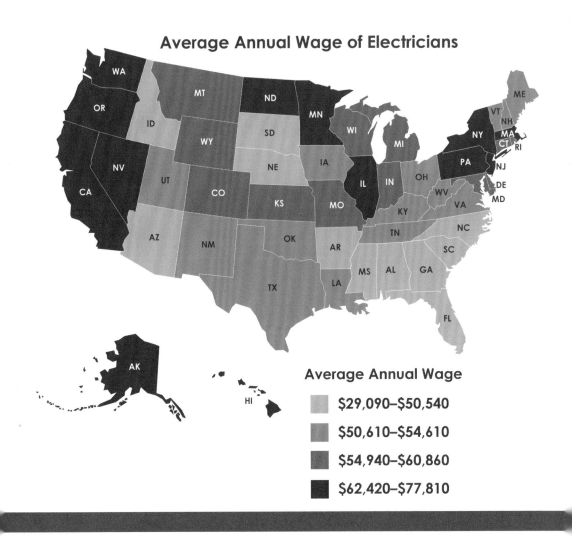

Average Annual Wage

- $29,090–$50,540
- $50,610–$54,610
- $54,940–$60,860
- $62,420–$77,810

US Bureau of Labor Statistics, "Annual Mean Wage of Electricians, by State, May 2018," Occupational Employment Statistics, *May 2018. www.bls.gov.*

a license if they pass. Electricians must

hold a license. This lets them work legally.

Each state has its own exam. But all states

require electricians to know the National Electrical Code. Electricians must also know local building codes.

Licensed electricians are called journey workers. Journey workers complete rough-in work on new construction sites. They also do a variety of repairs. Journey workers solve problems and keep customers happy.

Some people remain journey workers for their entire careers. In many states, they can work independently. They may also work as part of a company. As of 2018, the median wage for licensed electricians

Master electricians can manage larger projects. They are responsible for training apprentices.

was $55,190. This is more than $10,000

higher than the median wage for other

construction workers.

MASTER ELECTRICIANS

Some electricians decide they want to go further in their careers. They want to go from a journey worker to a master. To do this, they need additional experience and training. Each state's laws are different. In most cases, electricians need to have three to six years of experience as a journey worker. They may take additional classes at a trade school. In some cases, they must also hold a degree in electrical engineering. Then they can take an exam. If they pass, they get a license to work as a master electrician.

Masters can do more complex work than journey workers. They do more than the common on-site jobs. Masters may start their own electrical company. If the business grows, they can hire journey workers and

OTHER TYPES OF ELECTRICIANS

Construction is not the only industry that employs electricians. Ships have electrical systems that need repairs. Marine electricians make those repairs. Studios where television shows and movies are made also need electricians. These people set up and control the lighting systems there. These electricians are called gaffers. Offshore electricians are also in demand. They work on oil and gas rigs in the ocean.

apprentices. The master is responsible for these employees.

Masters have other tasks too. They are responsible for managing projects. They design electrical systems for buildings. They also obtain permits for electrical work. Local governments issue permits. The permits give electricians permission to work on specific projects. Master electricians are experts in their field. They also constantly give back. Masters share their experience with apprentices who work under them. When masters share their skills, they keep the trade strong.

CHAPTER THREE

WHAT IS LIFE LIKE AS AN ELECTRICIAN?

Most electricians work full-time. Full-time work is forty hours or more a week. This equals about eight hours a day. Electricians usually work during the daytime. Sometimes electricians also work overtime. This may happen when a construction project falls behind.

Electricians may have to work extra hours to keep a construction project on schedule.

Or an emergency might arise. In that case, electricians might be called to a jobsite on evenings or weekends.

Self-employed electricians are able to select jobs they want. They can create their own schedules.

EMPLOYMENT

About two-thirds of electricians work

for contractors. Contractors oversee

construction projects. They hire the workers that are needed to complete a job. Electricians who do not work for contractors may find jobs in factories or work for the government. They maintain equipment and electrical systems. They keep factories running safely and smoothly. Other electricians are self-employed. They find and complete jobs on their own.

According the Bureau of Labor Statistics (BLS), in 2018 about 6 percent of electricians were self-employed. Self-employment has many benefits. Electricians can set their own hours. They can choose which jobs they take. Self-employed electricians also have the potential to earn more money. But these benefits have a flip side. Self-employed electricians must continually find new projects. They must also advertise and build a good reputation for their business. They must do these tasks in addition to the electrical work.

COMMON TRAITS OF ELECTRICIANS

Electricians share many traits. Many of these traits are physical. Good eyesight is a must. Electricians rely on their eyes for much of their job. They must also be able to see colors clearly. That is because

Working as an electrician can be physically demanding. An electrician might need to climb a ladder or fit into small spaces.

wires are color coded. For example, red or black wires usually carry electricity from the power source into the building. White or gray wires carry electricity from the building back to the electrical panel. Being able to tell the difference is an important part of the job.

TOOLS FOR ELECTRICIANS

Electricians rely on a variety of tools to do their jobs. Some are common hand tools. These include screwdrivers, levels, and pliers. Electricians use many specialized tools too. Multimeters are handheld devices. They measure the electricity in a circuit. Fish tape is a long, narrow strip of steel. It allows electricians to run wire behind walls.

Many electricians also find it easier to do their jobs if they are fit. That is because electrical work can be physically demanding. Electricians are on their feet most of the day. The job may require them to move heavy tools and supplies. They may need to climb on ladders or crawl in attics to reach their work. Most electricians are also good at working with their hands. The job requires them to work with tools and small electrical parts.

Electricians need good people skills too. On an average day, electricians must speak with customers. Each customer is different. An electrician must be skilled at talking with a variety of people. The customer will explain what the problem is. Then electricians must clearly explain how they can fix it. They also say what the cost will be. People skills are important at construction sites too. Electricians need to speak with other trade workers. They may also have to communicate with managers and **foremen**.

Electricians need to be comfortable working in a variety of settings. Each day is different. "We start at about 6:30, get all together with all the guys, and you go

Electricians must be able to communicate well with customers and other trade workers.

over all the tasks you have for the day,"

says electrician Jeffrey Tyson.[6] They gather

the tools and supplies for that day's job.

Daily tasks change often. One day an

electrician may be working outside in

Working with electricity can be dangerous. If electricians are not careful, they can be electrocuted.

freezing weather. Another day he or she

might be inside running wires or installing

light switches. "It's a great environment

because you always have different things

going on," says Tyson.[7]

RISKS OF THE JOB

Being an electrician comes with risks.

Electricians have a greater chance of injury

than people in many other jobs. The most

obvious job hazard is electricity itself.

Electricity has the potential to be deadly.

Working with live wires is dangerous. Live

wires have electricity flowing through them.

CIRCUIT BREAKERS

A circuit breaker is a safety feature. Too much electricity may flow through a circuit. This overloads the circuit. An overloaded circuit can cause fires or other damage. Circuit breakers prevent this from happening. They turn off the circuit before it overloads.

Electricians must protect themselves with safety gear and tools.

Touching a live wire can lead to shocks, burns, and death.

Electricians are trained to follow many safety measures. One is called lockout/tagout. Lockout is putting a physical lock on a device. Devices include circuit breakers or switches. The lock prevents anyone from turning on the power. Tagout means placing a label on a device. The label warns of danger. It may say something like "Do not operate. Equipment locked out." These measures aim to prevent electricity-related accidents or injuries.

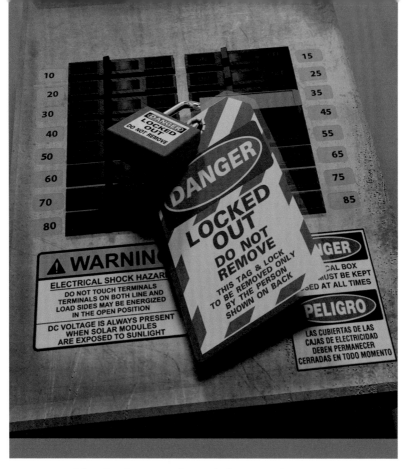

Tags and locks keep electricians safe. They protect electricians from electrocution.

Electricians face some of the same risks as other construction workers. They climb up and down ladders. Electricians might fall. Using the wrong tool for the job can cause accidents. For example, tools used near live wires must be **insulated**. Uninsulated tools can lead to serious injuries, such as electric shock. Old homes and buildings can be dangerous. They may have harmful substances. Electricians working there may be exposed to them. Mold, lead, and other toxic chemicals can cause health problems.

Though their job has risks, many electricians enjoy the work. It is a career filled with variety and new challenges each day. It allows the electricians to work with their hands as well as their minds. For many electricians, these qualities create an ideal job.

CHAPTER FOUR

WHAT IS THE FUTURE FOR ELECTRICIANS?

The future for electrician jobs looks good. The BLS projects job growth. It estimates that electrician jobs are going to increase. Between 2018 and 2028, they could increase by 10 percent. That is about 74,000 new jobs. This rate of growth is higher than the average growth for all jobs.

Job opportunities for new electricians are growing. There will be many new types of jobs for electricians in the future.

LABOR SHORTAGE

Part of the growth is due to labor shortage.

Many jobs are available for electricians.

As older electricians retire, not enough young electricians are replacing them.

But there are not enough electricians to do all the work. Contractors must turn down jobs. They do not have enough electricians. According to the BLS, there will be nearly 86,000 unfilled electrician jobs by 2024.

Many electricians are retiring. Not enough new electricians are being trained. Paul Pompeo sees this problem every day. He is the president of the Pompeo Group. It is a company that hires electricians for projects across the country. Pompeo says that "many baby boomers are hitting retirement age." Baby boomers are people who were

---

ELECTRICIANS AND THE ECONOMY

Job growth for electricians is tied closely to the economy. In a strong economy, construction usually booms. Electricians have lots of work. If the economy slows, then construction usually slows too. Electricians have less work. Employment is most stable for electricians who work in factories. These jobs are less affected by changes in the economy.

born between 1946 and 1964. When they retire, most leave the industry full-time. Because of this, Pompeo says, "we definitely need to add more people into the pipeline to meet the demand."[8]

ATTRACTING NEW ELECTRICIANS

Attracting new electricians is not easy. Trade school has become a less popular option. This has happened over the past several decades. Many high schools push students to go to four-year colleges. They push this instead of learning a trade. Some people believe trade schools are only for students who struggle in school.

"Many students . . . may not even be familiar with trade professions," says John Donahue.[9] He works as a director of the IBEW-NECA Technical Institute. It is a trade school in Chicago, Illinois.

SHIFTS IN EDUCATION

For years, many students felt their only option was college. They chose college over trade schools. A shortage of trade workers grew. This gap created job opportunities. The opportunities renewed interest in trade schools. Enrollment grew from 9.6 million students in 1999 to 16 million in 2014. "It's a cultural rebuild," says Randy Emery. Emery is a welding instructor at the College of the Sequoias in California.

Quoted in Matt Krupnick, "After Decades of Pushing Bachelor's Degrees, US Needs More Tradespeople," PBS News Hour, *August 29, 2017. www.pbs.org/newshour.*

Some high school programs introduce students to electrical work.

The institute has a project called Chicago Builds. It began in Chicago public schools in 2016. It trains high school students in construction. "We provide teaching assistance and a curriculum," says Donahue. "After an introduction to the construction industry in general, we move into electrical work."[10] The program teaches material identification. It shows how to use tools. It also provides hands-on activities.

Program leaders have high hopes for training like this. They hope hands-on work will excite students. Then the students will want to become electricians. Leaders also hope that teachers will be role models.

One of those teachers is Mario Miller. He grew up in Chicago. He teaches at Dunbar High School. "These kids may come from a disadvantaged or poor background," says Miller. "They see me, a black electrician. I'm someone who looks like them with relatable circumstances, and I have this successful career. That, itself, is influential and opens their minds to the possibility of [the] profession and avenues to success."[11]

GROWING INDUSTRIES

New electricians will have many job options. Electricians have traditionally worked in

Wind energy is a growing industry that can create many jobs for electricians.

More opportunities are arising in renewable energy, such as solar energy.

construction. But new technologies are changing that. This is especially true in the area of renewable energy. Renewable energy generates power from wind and sunlight. More and more companies work in renewable energy. Electricians can connect these new power sources to the power grid. Then homes and businesses can use that energy.

The renewable energy industry is growing. Wind power made up 6.5 percent of the nation's electricity in 2018. The Department of Energy (DOE) estimates this could increase. It could be 20 percent by 2030. The DOE began working toward that goal in 2008. "It will take a huge amount of effort to reach this goal, but if we're successful, we'll be able to create hundreds of thousands of jobs for electricians and electrical contractors," said Jim Johnson.[12] He was a senior engineer at the time. He worked for the DOE's Wind Technology Center Program.

Solar energy is also growing. It is the fastest-growing area of renewable energy. As of 2019, more than 2 million solar power installations existed in the United States. Electricians connect homes to solar power.

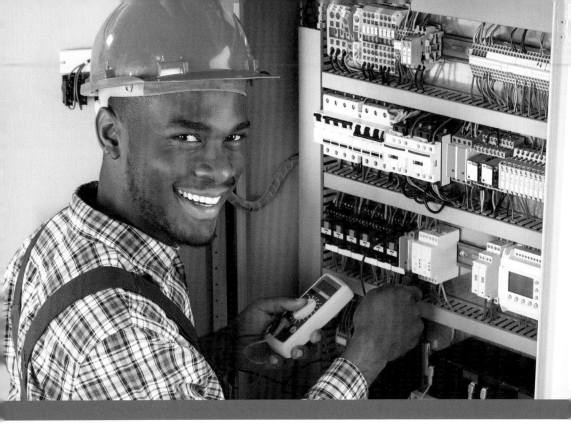

In the future, there will be many career opportunities for electricians.

Energy sources may change over time. What will not change is the need for electricians. People count on electricity to keep their homes and businesses working. They rely on electricians to keep these systems running smoothly.

GLOSSARY

circuits

closed paths through which electricity can flow

economy

the condition of a country's goods and services

foremen

people who oversee workers at a job site

high voltage

describing a powerful flow of electricity

insulated

describing a tool with a handle that is covered in thick layers of rubber and plastic to prevent electricity from passing through it

license

legal permission to do something

power surges

spikes of energy in electrical currents

transformers

devices that change the voltage of electric currents

unions

organizations of workers formed to protect their working conditions, pay, and health benefits

SOURCE NOTES

INTRODUCTION: WHY BECOME AN ELECTRICIAN?

1. Quoted in Claire Swedberg, "Family Ties," *Electrical Contractor*, March 2006. www.ecmag.com.

2. Quoted in Swedberg, "Family Ties."

CHAPTER ONE: WHAT DOES AN ELECTRICIAN DO?

3. Quoted in "Day in the Life of an Electrician," *YouTube*, uploaded by Electrical Contractors Association of Alberta, February 27, 2018. www.youtube.com.

4. Quoted in "Day in the Life of an Electrician."

5. Quoted in Tonia Nifong, "A Day in the Life of an Electrician: Michael Lucas," *The Electrical Blog*, Berwick Electric Co., October 16, 2013. www.berwickelectric.com.

CHAPTER THREE: WHAT IS LIFE LIKE AS AN ELECTRICIAN?

6. Quoted in "Day in the Life of an Electrician."

7. Quoted in "Day in the Life of an Electrician."

CHAPTER FOUR: WHAT IS THE FUTURE FOR ELECTRICIANS?

8. Quoted in Susan Bloom, "Moving the Needle," *Electrical Contractor*, February 2019. www.ecmag.com.

9. Quoted in Jeff Gavin, "Stemming the Tide," *Electrical Contractor*, September 2017. www.ecmag.com.

10. Quoted in Gavin, "Stemming the Tide."

11. Quoted in Gavin, "Stemming the Tide."

12. Quoted in Amy Florence Fischbach, "Winds of Change," *EC&M*, January 1, 2009. www.ecmweb.com.

FOR FURTHER RESEARCH

BOOKS

Heidi Ayarbe, *Electricians on the Job*. Mankato, MN: The Child's World, 2020.

W. L. Kitts, *Great Jobs in the Skilled Trades*. San Diego, CA: ReferencePoint Press, 2019.

Ellen Labrecque, *Renewable Energy*. Ann Arbor, MI: Cherry Lake Publishing, 2018.

INTERNET SOURCES

Bureau of Labor Statistics, "Electricians," *Occupational Outlook Handbook*, US Department of Labor, December 3, 2019. www.bls.gov.

"Electricity," *DK FindOut!*, n.d. www.dkfindout.com.

WEBSITES

Apprenticeship.gov
www.apprenticeship.gov

Apprenticeship.gov is a part of the US Department of Labor. This website provides information about apprenticeships. People can find and apply to apprenticeships through the website.

Electrical Training Alliance
www.electricaltrainingalliance.org

The Electrical Training Alliance is a training organization endorsed by electrical unions. In more than seventy years of operation, it has trained more than 350,000 electricians.

Independent Electrical Contractors (IEC)
www.ieci.org

IEC is one of the nation's largest associations of electricians. It has more than fifty-two chapters in the United States. It trains more than 12,000 apprentice electricians each year.

INDEX

IMAGE CREDITS

ABOUT THE AUTHOR

Kate Conley has been writing nonfiction books for children for more than a decade. When she's not writing, Conley spends her time reading, drawing, and solving crossword puzzles. She lives in Minnesota with her husband and two children.